W9-BPS-864

Animal Homes

Published in the United States by Kingfisher,
175 Fifth Ave., New York, NY 10010
Kingfisher is an imprint of Macmillan Children's Books, London.

First published as *Kingfisher Young Knowledge: Animal Homes* in 2003
Additional material produced for Kingfisher by Discovery Books Ltd.

Distributed in the U.S. and Canada by Macmillan,
175 Fifth Ave., New York, NY 10010

Library of Congress Cataloging-in-Publication data has been applied for.

ISBN: 978-0-7534-6775-6

Kingfisher books are available for special promotions and premiums.
For details contact: Special Markets Department, Macmillan,
175 Fifth Ave., New York, NY 10010.

For more information, please visit www.kingfisherbooks.com

Printed in China
1 3 5 7 9 8 6 4 2
1TR/1211/UTD/WKT/140MA

Note to readers: the website addresses listed in this book are correct at the time of going to print. However, due to the ever-changing nature of the Internet, website addresses and content can change. Websites can contain links that are unsuitable for children. The publisher cannot be held responsible for changes in website addresses or content or for information obtained through a third party. We strongly advise that Internet searches should be supervised by an adult.

Acknowledgments

The publisher would like to thank the following for permission to reproduce their material. Every care has been taken to trace copyright holders. However, if there have been unintentional omissions or failure to trace copyright holders, we apologize and will, if informed, endeavor to make corrections in any future edition.

b = bottom, *c* = center, *l* = left, *t* = top, *r* = right

Cover: all images courtesy of Shutterstock.com; 4–5 National Geographic Image Collection; 8 Oxford Scientific Films (OSF); 9*t* OSF; 9*b* OSF; 10 OSF; 11*t* Getty Images; 11*b* OSF; 12–13 Getty Images; 13*c* Corbis; 14 Corbis; 15*t* Corbis; 15*b* Corbis; 16 Nature Picture Library; 18*tl* Nature Picture Library; 18–19 National Geographic Image Collection; 19*t* Getty Images; 21 Ardea; 22*tr* Nature Picture Library; 22*b* Natural History Picture Agency (NHPA); 23*t* Corbis; 23*b* Nature Picture Library; 26 Corbis; 27 Ardea; 28–29 National Geographic Image Collection; 29*t* Corbis; 30*bl* OSF; 31*t* Corbis; 31*b* Ardea; 32*t* NHPA; 32–33 NHPA; 33*b* NHPA; 35*t* NHPA; 36 Corbis; 36–37 Still Pictures; 37 OSF; 38 Corbis; 38–39 Getty Images; 39 Nature Picture Library; 48*t* Shutterstock Images/Steve Bower; 48*b* Shutterstock Images/FloridaStock; 49 National Park Service; 52 Shutterstock Images/DGF72; 53*t* Shutterstock Images/Csati; 53*b* Shutterstock Images/Muslov Dmitry; 56 Shutterstock Images/picturepartners

Commissioned photography on pages 42–47 by Andy Crawford
Thank you to models Eleanor Davis, Lewis Manu, Daniel Newton, Lucy Newton, Nikolas Omilana, and Olivia Omilana

discover science

Animal Homes

Angela Wilkes

KINGFISHER
NEW YORK

Contents

What is a home?

Animals need homes for all of the same reasons that people do. Homes provide shelter and keep animals warm in the winter. They are a safe place to rest and raise babies.

Hard to find

Animals build their homes out of materials that match their surroundings. This makes it hard for predators to spot them.

Safe place for babies

Homes such as this bird's nest are built only for raising babies. A nest is warm, snug, and out of the reach of danger. This is where a mother bird lays her eggs and brings up her young.

Different homes

Animals make many kinds of homes. Some build nests, while others make dens or dig burrows.

Living in a pond

Many different animals live in the still, fresh water of a pond. There they can find good hiding places and many things to eat.

Finding a mate

Newts live in ponds in the spring. They look for a mate and then lay their eggs in the water.

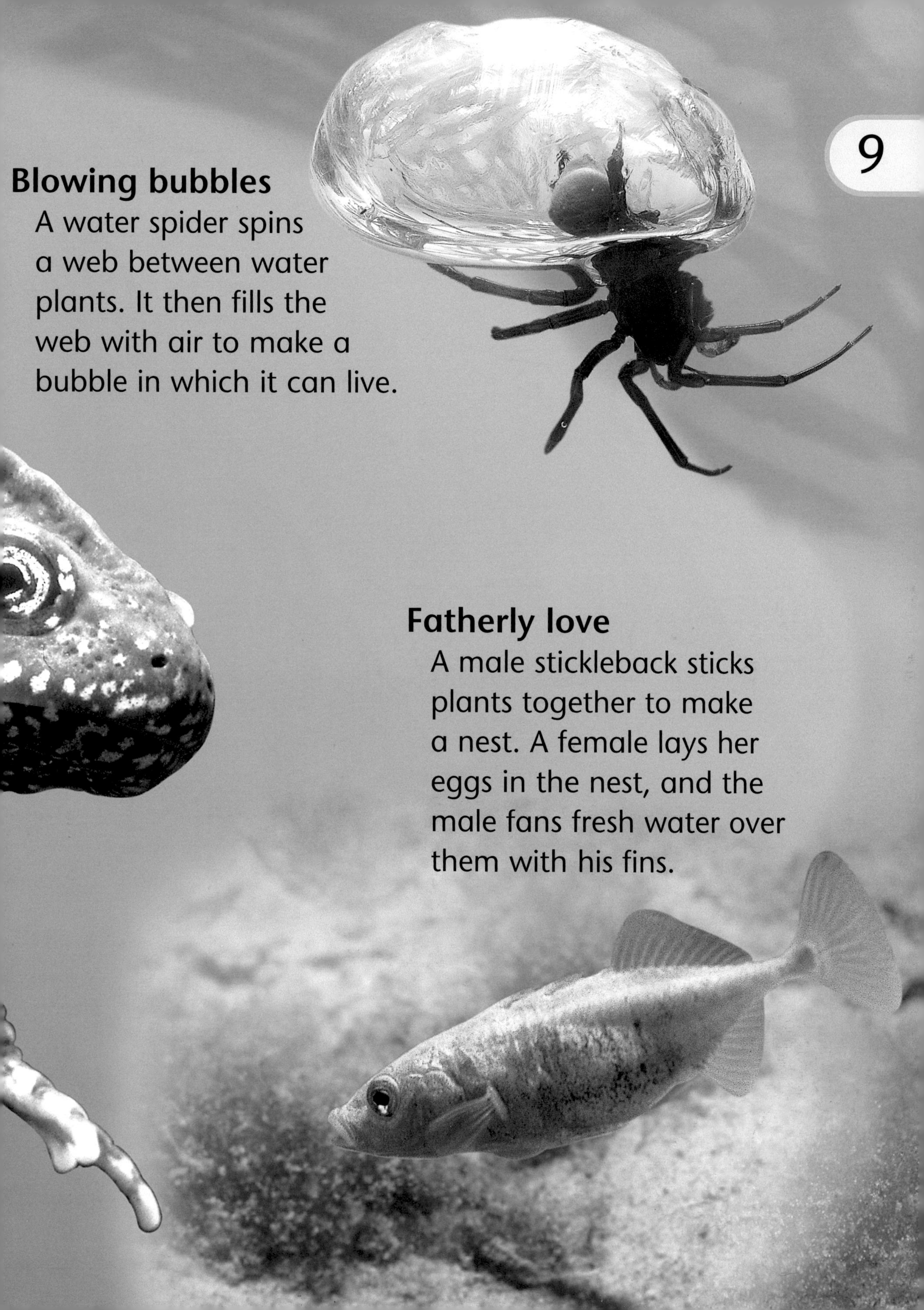

Blowing bubbles

A water spider spins a web between water plants. It then fills the web with air to make a bubble in which it can live.

Fatherly love

A male stickleback sticks plants together to make a nest. A female lays her eggs in the nest, and the male fans fresh water over them with his fins.

Staying damp

Amphibians, such as frogs and toads, live in damp, shady places. They need to keep their skin moist and slimy. Some make their homes in unusual spots.

Living in a hole

When it rains, a water-holding frog's skin soaks up water. The slime on its skin sets to make a cocoon that keeps in the water. The frog then burrows into the sand to escape the desert heat.

water-holding frog

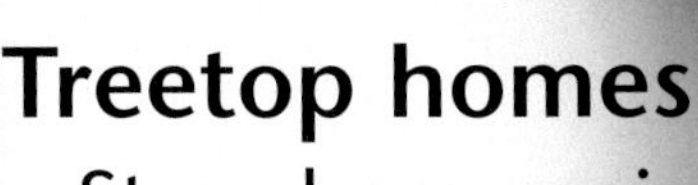

Treetop homes

Strawberry poison-arrow frogs live in steamy rainforests. They hide from the hot sun in pools of rainwater that collect in the middle of huge plants.

Burrowing toads

Spadefoot toads dig burrows and spend most of their time in them. But when it rains, they come above the ground to find mates.

Mobile homes

Some animals live in a shell that they carry on their back. The hard shell shields an animal's soft body from knocks and bumps and shelters it from the wind and rain. It also protects it from hungry predators looking for food.

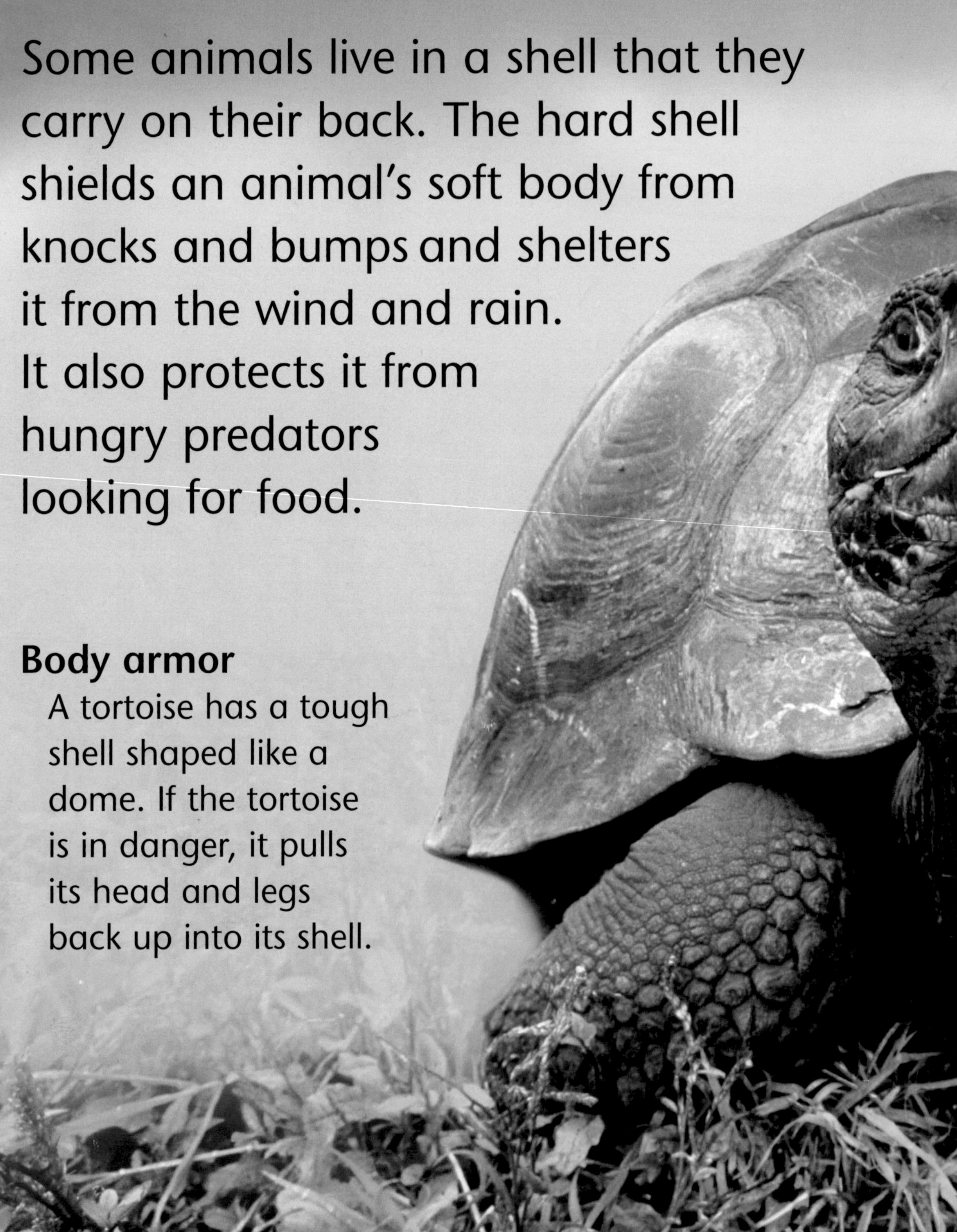

Body armor

A tortoise has a tough shell shaped like a dome. If the tortoise is in danger, it pulls its head and legs back up into its shell.

A home that grows

As a snail grows, its shell grows, too, so the shell is always exactly the right size. Snails slide back inside their shells to hide from danger.

Borrowed home

A hermit crab has no hard shell of its own, so it finds an empty mollusk shell and moves in. When the hermit crab grows, it moves to a bigger shell.

Spinning webs

Most spiders spin webs to catch insects. They build them out of silk threads from their own bodies. But some spiders live in other types of homes, such as holes or burrows.

Cobweb trap

An orb-weaver spider spins a beautiful sticky web between the stems of plants. The spider lies in wait for insects in the center of the web or hides under a nearby leaf.

Under a rock

Some spiders make nests in hollows under rocks. They line the nests with thick silk and lay their eggs. Then they wait to pounce on passing insects.

Ambush!

A trapdoor spider digs a tunnel and lines it with silk. Then it makes a lid on top, like a trapdoor. The spider hides in the tunnel and darts out to catch prey.

16 Where birds live

Birds build nests so that they have a warm, safe place to lay their eggs and raise their chicks. Most birds' nests are in trees, but some are on steep cliffs or even on the ground.

Hanging nest

A penduline tit hangs its purse-shaped nest from a twig. It is lined with soft wool and fluff from reeds or catkins to make a cozy home for the female and babies.

Fancy work

A male cape weaverbird weaves a complicated oval nest out of grass and reeds. The only way in is through a short tunnel at the bottom. This helps protect it from predators.

Hungry chicks

Chicks hatch in their nest. They are helpless and cannot leave. They open their beaks wide to beg for food.

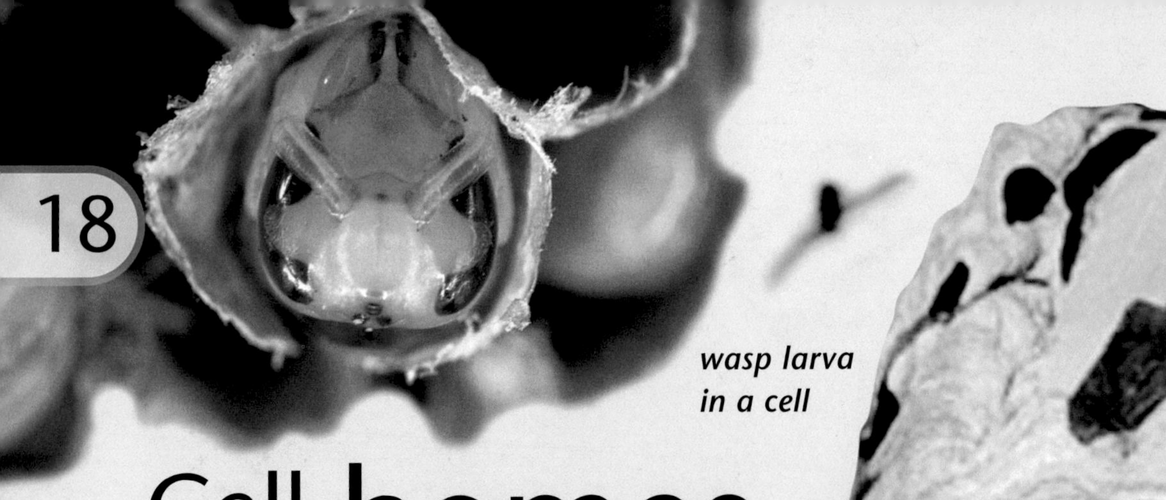

wasp larva in a cell

Cell homes

Wasps and bees build fantastic nests made up of many tiny cells. Young wasps and bees can grow up safely inside these little compartments.

Laying eggs

A queen wasp lays one egg in each cell. Each egg will become a wasp larva. Older wasps look after the eggs and larvae.

Paper home

A wasp's nest is made of layers of paper wrapped around the larvae cells. The wasps make paper by chewing up wood and mixing it with their spit.

Moving around

Bees live and work together. When bees need a new home, they fly away in a huge group called a swarm.

Honeycomb homes

Bees' nests are called hives. Inside a hive are wax honeycombs made of many cells. The cells hold honey or baby bees.

leafcutter ants

Living in a colony

Most ants and termites live in huge groups called colonies. They work together to build enormous nests in which to raise their young.

Food for the colony

Leafcutter ants live in rainforests. They bite off pieces of leaves and carry them back to their nest. They store the leaves in special gardens, where a fungus grows on them, making a tasty food for the ants.

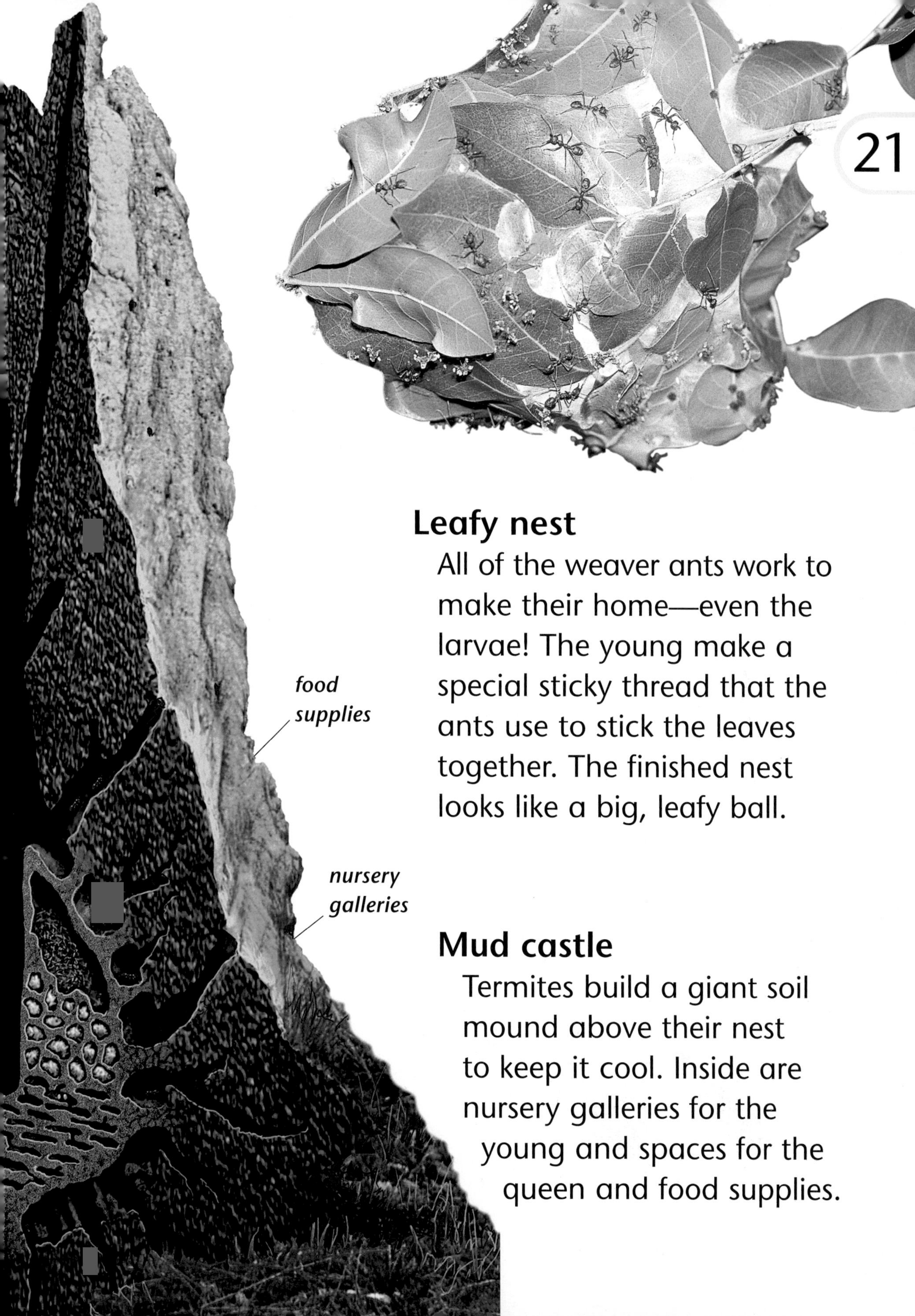

Leafy nest

All of the weaver ants work to make their home—even the larvae! The young make a special sticky thread that the ants use to stick the leaves together. The finished nest looks like a big, leafy ball.

Mud castle

Termites build a giant soil mound above their nest to keep it cool. Inside are nursery galleries for the young and spaces for the queen and food supplies.

Mini homes

Mice live in many places. Some live in fields, and some live in forests. Others even live in people's homes. But all mice build nests to rest in and bring up their babies.

Close to people

House mice make their nests from shredded paper, old rags, or grass. They always build them in a small hiding place well out of sight.

Grassy home

A tiny harvest mouse lives in tall grass. It weaves strips of grass around plant stems to make a snug, round nest.

Sleepy mouse

In the fall, a dormouse makes a cozy nest out of shredded bark. Then it curls up into a ball and goes to sleep for the long, cold winter.

24 Under the ground

Marmots live high up in the mountains. When the first winter snow falls, the whole family moves into a big burrow lined with grass and goes to sleep.

Fast asleep

The marmots block the entrance to the burrow with rocks and soil to stop predators from getting in. Then they snuggle together for warmth and hibernate until spring comes again.

Where dogs live

Foxes and dingoes are wild dogs. They make their homes by digging dens in soft soil or by taking over and enlarging the homes of other animals. Dens provide shelter from the hot sun or cold weather and are a safe place to bring up pups.

Desert homes
Kit foxes live in stony deserts in North America. They sleep in their dens during the day, when the sun is at its hottest. At night, when it is cooler, they go out hunting.

Ready-made den

Dingoes live in Australia. When a mother dingo is about to have pups, she moves into a safe den. This is often a big hole beneath some rocks or tree roots.

28 Living in the snow

Polar bears live in the snowy Arctic. When they are tired, they dig a shallow pit in the snow and sleep in it. In the fall, a pregnant polar bear digs a den in a snowdrift. This is where she will spend the long, dark winter.

Snow babies

A mother bear stays in the den until the spring. In the early winter, she gives birth to one or two cubs. She feeds them her milk, and they all sleep for most of the winter.

Leaving the den

In the spring, the polar bear and her young come out of the den. The mother is very hungry because she has not eaten all winter. She takes her cubs onto the sea ice, where she can hunt for food.

Going batty

Bats go out hunting for food at night and rest during the day. They do not make special homes but roost in trees, caves, barns, or even attics.

Leafy shelter

Fruit bats live in huge groups called colonies and roost in tall trees during the day. They hang upside down from branches, clinging on tightly with the claws on their feet. Then they wrap their skinny wings around themselves for protection.

Dark caves

Many bats sleep in large caves. Thousands of them roost upside down, packed closely together. When evening comes, the bats set out to feed. Some bats feed on insects. Others, such as these flying foxes, eat fruit and the nectar from flowers.

dragonfly

Riverside homes

Many animals live on the banks of rivers and streams. There they are close to fresh water, and there are plenty of plants, small creatures, and fish to eat. They are also safely out of the reach of most predators.

Water babies

Adult dragonflies live beside rivers. The larvae live in the water. When the larvae are ready to become adults, they climb up a plant's stem. Their skin splits open along their backs, and the adult dragonflies climb out.

Nest tunnel

Kingfishers dig a tunnel in a soft riverbank. At the end of the tunnel, a female kingfisher makes a small chamber and lays her eggs. When the chicks hatch, she brings them fish to eat.

Nesting burrow

Platypuses live near lakes and rivers. A mother platypus digs a long nesting burrow in the soft soil of the bank. There she lays her eggs and takes care of her babies.

34 Living in a lodge

Beavers are smart builders. They construct dams across streams to make ponds. Then they build homes called lodges in the middle of these ponds.

Safe from enemies

The beavers line the lodge with dry grass to keep it snug and warm. All of the entrances are underwater, safe from predators.

Timber!

Using their sharp front teeth, beavers can cut down trees. They gnaw around the bottom of a tree until it falls down. Then they chew pieces off to make small logs.

Saving food for later

Beavers eat only plants. They store some food at the bottom of the pond so that they can eat all winter.

Going camping

Big apes, such as chimpanzees, orangutans, and gorillas, do not have one home. They move from place to place. At night, they make leafy nests and camp out.

Climbing trees

Chimpanzees make tree nests at nighttime. They bend leafy branches to make comfortable beds on which they can sleep.

Leafy nests

Orangutans make two tree nests a day. They make a small nest for a nap, and at night, they build platforms in the forks of trees.

Heavy sleepers

Female gorillas nest in trees. Male gorillas make nests on the ground, as they are too heavy to sleep in trees!

Living with people

Towns and cities offer shelter, food, and warmth. As they have grown in size, more animals have moved into them. Animals often settle into new homes in the most surprising places.

Cardboard bed
In North America, raccoons have moved to town parks and even downtown areas. They live in attics and sheds. Raccoons eat almost anything and even help themselves to food from garbage cans!

Living the high life

The peregrine falcon usually lives on cliff or rock faces. In cities, it roosts on churches, tall buildings, and even radio masts.

Chimney homes

For hundreds of years, the white stork has nested close to people. It makes its huge nest on top of chimneys and houses. Some people build special platforms for storks to nest on.

Looking at homes

You will need:

- Plastic cup
- Scissors
- Plastic wrap
- Rubber bands

Make a pond viewer

With this simple underwater viewer, you can take a closer look at the small creatures that live in ponds and streams.

Hold the plastic cup firmly in one hand. Then hold the scissors in your other hand and carefully cut out the bottom of the cup.

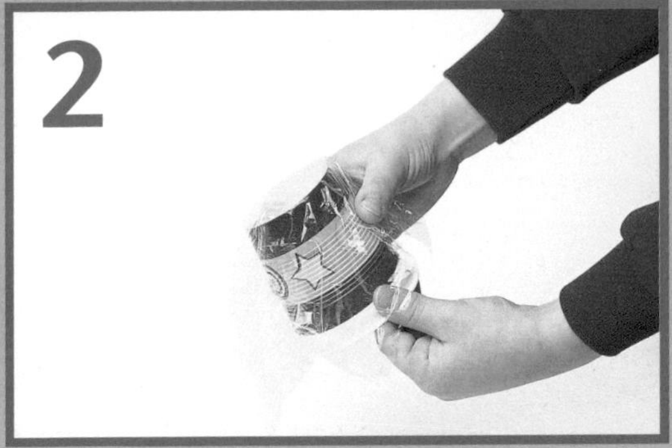

Cut out a large circle of plastic wrap. Stretch it tightly over the cutoff end of the cup until the plastic wrap is smooth.

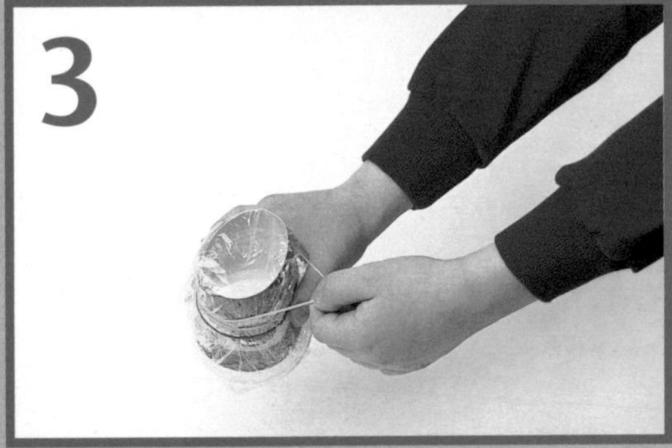

Stretch a couple of rubber bands over the plastic wrap to hold it in place. Pull the edges of the plastic wrap tight again.

To use the pond viewer, dip the end covered with plastic wrap into the water. Then look through the open end at the top of the cup.

Make a nest

Watch different birds making their nests in the spring. See if you can copy them by making a bird's nest of your own.

You will need:
- Paintbrush and glue
- Plastic bowl
- Dried grass
- Moss
- Feathers and leaves
- Candy wrappers

Using a paintbrush, spread glue all around the outside of the bowl. Pick up small handfuls of dried grass and stick them onto the bowl.

Spread glue around the inside of the bowl. Then stick on a layer of more dried grass and moss to make a soft, cozy middle.

Scatter a few small feathers and leaves inside the nest to make it look realistic. Decorate it with candy wrappers to add color.

42 Watching animals

Make a tepee hideout

If you make a simple tepee in your yard or local park, you can hide inside it and watch animals.

You will need:

- Large sheet
- Poster paints
- Paintbrush
- 4 bamboo canes
- Garden twine
- Scissors

1

Mix the paints with a little water so that they are easy to use. Paint circles and other bold shapes on the sheet. Leave the sheet to dry.

2

Stand the four bamboo canes together and make them into a tepee shape. Cut a long piece of twine and tie the canes firmly together at the top.

Wrap the sheet around the tepee frame. Tie it in place at the top of the canes with more twine.

See where your face comes up to on the sheet. Cut out a peephole big enough for you to see out of.

Go inside the tepee hideout and close the loose edges of the sheet behind you. Stay as quiet and still as you can and wait to see which animals come close. Take a notebook and pencil so that you can write down what you see.

Making homes

Make a hermit crab

Make a crab out of modeling clay and put it in an empty shell. Then it will be just like a real hermit crab.

You will need:
- Modeling clay
- Shell
- Pipecleaner

Roll two pieces of modeling clay into balls for the crab's head and body. Make four small sausages for legs and two claw shapes.

Break off two tiny pieces of a different color of modeling clay. Roll them into small balls for the eyes and stick them onto the head.

Stick the head, claws, and legs to the crab's body. Make feelers from two pieces of pipecleaner and then put the crab in the shell.

Flowerpot home

Make a home for creepy-crawlies. Check to see what is inside it every day and draw the creatures you find there.

You will need:
- Flowerpot
- Small rock
- Notebook and pen

1

Ask an adult to help you find a shady spot somewhere near your home. Turn the flowerpot upside down and prop it up on the rock.

2

After a few days, look inside the flowerpot. Draw pictures in your notebook of any creatures you find. Can you name them?

Bee home

Make this simple bee box and hang it in a sunny place outside. The straws should slope down inside the bottle.

You will need:
- Scissors
- Large plastic bottle
- Drinking straws
- String

Cut off the top end off the bottle and fill it with straws. Then tie string around the bottle and hang it up outside.

Hamster fun box

Build a fun box

Your pet hamster or mouse will have a lot of fun with this play box. It can climb in and out of it, as if on a jungle gym.

You will need:

- Shoebox
- 4 cardboard tubes
- Pencil
- Scissors
- Poster paints
- Paintbrush
- Plastic cup

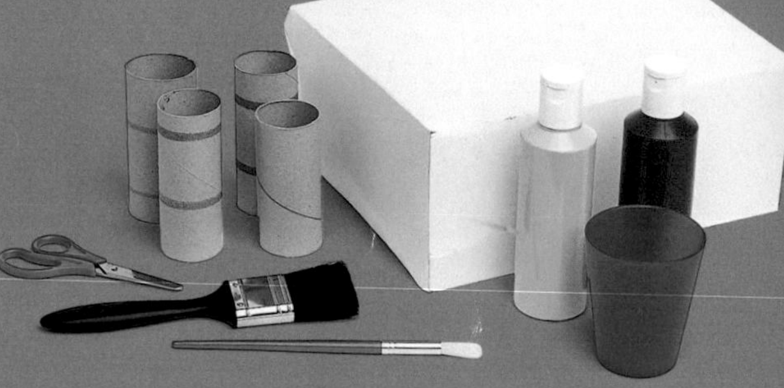

Position a cardboard tube in the middle of one end of the shoebox and trace around it. Repeat on the other sides of the box.

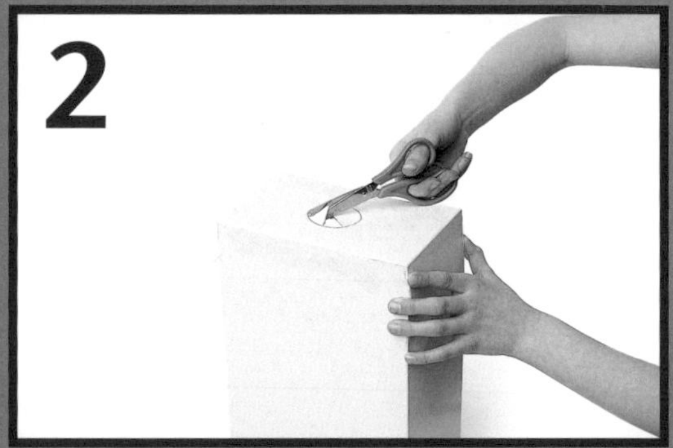

Make a hole in the center of one circle and cut out lines to the edge of it. Then cut out the circle. Do this with all of the circles on the box.

Mix some poster paint with a little water and carefully paint the cardboard box all over. Then leave the paint to dry.

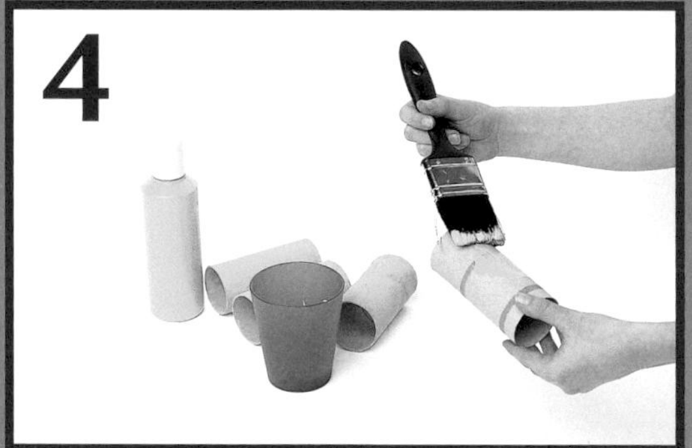

Paint the cardboard tubes a different color. Paint one end of each tube and let it dry. Then paint the other half of the tube and leave that to dry, too.

Push the cardboard tubes into the holes around the sides of the box. They should fit firmly and stick out a little. Now see if your hamster wants to play.

Glossary

amphibian—an animal that is born in the water but grows up to live on land as well

ape—an animal that looks like a monkey without a tail

bark—the outer layer of a tree's trunk or branches

catkin—a spike of small, soft flowers on a tree

chamber—a room

cocoon—a wrapping that protects an animal

colony—a group of animals that live together

dam—a barrier built across a valley to hold back water

den—a sheltered place where an animal lives

enlarging—making bigger

fungus—a plant, such as a toadstool, that grows on other plants

gallery—a long room or passage

hibernate—to spend the entire winter in a deep sleep

larva—a young insect that has just come out of its egg

larvae—more than one larva

mollusk—an animal with a soft body and a hard shell

nectar—a liquid produced by flowers and collected by insects

platform—a flat surface

predator—an animal that hunts and eats other animals

pregnant—going to have a baby

prey—an animal that is hunted and killed by another animal

roost—to settle down to sleep

sea ice—ice that forms on the surface of the ocean or sea when it freezes

shield—to protect and take care of

shredded—torn into pieces

snowdrift—a large pile of snow that has been heaped up by the wind

swarm—a large group of insects flying together

Parent and teacher notes

The content of this book can be used to teach, reinforce, and enhance many components of the science and language arts curricula. It also provides opportunities for crosscurricular connections, especially in math, geography, and art.

Extension activities

Writing and oral language
Select an animal and write a news article reporting on the process and success of building its home. Present your article as a news broadcast.

Creative writing
One night when a huge colony of bats goes out hunting (pp. 30–31), a young bat gets separated from the others. Write a short story about its adventures and how it eventually finds its way back to the colony.

Using graphic organizers
Select two animals featured in this book. Use a Venn diagram to show the similarities and differences between how each one builds and uses its home. For example, draw two circles that overlap in the middle on a piece of paper. Label one "Harvest mouse" and the other "Cape weaverbird." In the harvest mouse circle, you could write, "Has several openings" and for the cape weaverbird, "One opening." Then in the overlapping area you can write down points about the homes that are similar—for example, "Woven."

Science
The study of animal homes relates to scientific themes of behavior, diversity, structure and function, survival, and interaction with the environment. Some specific links to the science curriculum include adaptations (pp. 9–13, 18–21, 30, 35); predator-prey relationships (pp. 12–15, 17, 34); growth and development (pp. 17–21, 26–29, 32–33); habitats (pp. 7–11, 15–16, 20–39); reproduction (pp. 6–9, 18, 28, 33); and food chains (pp. 31–33, 35, 38).

Crosscurricular links
1) Math: Make a list of 15–20 different animals whose homes are described in this book. Create a bar graph to show how many homes are above the ground, on the ground, beneath the ground, or in the water.

2) Geography: Make a list of at least six different mammals found in this book. Find where in the world they build their homes.

Using the projects
Children can do these projects at home. Here are some ideas for extending them:

Pages 40–41: Take a walk through a park or bushy area to look for spider webs. Make drawings or take photographs of any webs you see.

Pages 42–43: To watch smaller animals, such as insects or creatures that live in a pond, creek, or tidal pool, find a good place to sit and remain very still. In time, the animals will get used to you being there and will move around as usual.

Pages 44–45: Build a potato house. Have an adult help you cut a large baking potato in half lengthwise. Scoop out the insides, leaving about half an inch (1 centimeter) inside the skin. Cut a notch in one end of each potato half. Place the halves, with the scooped-out side down, under a plant or in the grass. Check every day to see who may have moved in.

Pages 46–47: Use a shoebox to make a home for a caterpillar. Make some small air holes in the sides with a sharp pencil. When you collect your caterpillar, make a note of the plant it's eating and keep fresh leaves from this plant in the box. Some caterpillars are picky eaters! Put a small branch inside for the caterpillar to climb on when it is ready to spin a cocoon and turn into a moth or butterfly.

52 Did you know?

- When a polar bear cub is born, it cannot see or hear for about a month.
- A platypus can consume its own body weight in food in 24 hours.
- The female potter wasp stuffs her nest with dead spiders and caterpillars before sealing it shut with mud. The creatures provide food for her larvae when they hatch.
- The male satin bowerbird collects feathers, shells, and other colorful bits and pieces to attract a female to its nest.
- The bee hummingbird makes its nest from spider webs and bark scraps.
- The roof of the nest of the hamerkop, an African bird, is so strong that it can hold the weight of a human being.

- The largest wasp nest on record was found in New Zealand and measured 11.8 feet (3.6 meters) long, with a diameter of 5.9 feet (1.8 meters)!
- Prairie dogs stand guard at the entrance to their burrows. When they spot danger, they bark a warning so that the other prairie dogs can rush inside to safety.
- The cave swiftlet builds its nest using saliva. It can take up to two months to build.
- Termites are tiny, but their mounds can be taller than a human.
- The desert tortoise spends more than nine-tenths of its life in a burrow.
- Some spiders in the Americas build their webs and join them to their neighbor's web. With one huge web, they can catch more prey.
- Kingfishers stab at the riverbank with their sharp beaks to make a tunnel to lay their eggs in.
- Tent-building bats make their homes out of large leaves. They nibble them along the center so that the leaves drop down around them, like a tent.

Animal homes quiz

The answers to these questions can all be found by looking back through the book. See how many you get right. You can check your answers on page 56.

1) How many eggs does a queen wasp lay in each cell of her nest?
A—Three
B—One
C—Two

2) What do marmots block their burrow entrance with?
A—Grass and straw
B—Rocks and soil
C—Sand

3) Where does the white stork build its nest?
A—In a tree
B—On the ground
C—On top of chimneys and houses

4) What does a tortoise do when it is in danger?
A—Run away
B—Roll over onto its back
C—Pull its head and legs back inside its shell

5) What is the name given to the place where termites look after their young?
A—Baby galleries
B—Nursery galleries
C—Grub galleries

6) Where does a beaver live?
A—A den
B—A nest
C—A lodge

7) How many nests can orangutans build in one day?
A—Five
B—Two
C—One

8) How does the water spider survive underwater?
A—It spins a web and makes an air bubble.
B—It comes up to the surface to breathe.
C—It gets oxygen from plants under the water.

9) What shape is the cape weaverbird's nest?
A—Square
B—Round
C—Oval

10) When do kit foxes hunt?
A—In the daytime
B—At night
C—Both during the day and at night

11) Where do male gorillas sleep?
A—In a tree
B—In a nest
C—On the ground

12) What is a flying group of bees called?
A—A hive
B—A swarm
C—A herd

Find out more

Books to read

Animals Building Homes (First Facts: Animal Behavior) by Wendy Perkins, Capstone Press, 2004

Ask Dr. K. Fisher about Animals by Claire Llewellyn, Kingfisher, 2007

Do Turtles Sleep in Treetops? A Book about Animal Homes (Animals All Around) by Laura Purdie Salas, Picture Window Books, 2007

Whose House Is This?: A Look at Animal Homes—Webs, Nests, and Shells by Elizabeth Gregoire, Picture Window Books, 2005

Places to visit

Philadelphia Zoo, Philadelphia, Pennsylvania
www.philadelphiazoo.org
Have a great day out at America's first zoo. Primates scoot around in the Treetop Trail above you while a snow leopard and red panda lurk in the Carnivore Kingdom—see if you can spot them! You can pet the friendly goats and sheep, feed the ducks, and much more in the Children's Zoo.

San Diego Zoo, San Diego, California
www.sandiegozoo.org
Visit the Urban Jungle, go exploring in the Outback, and delve deep into the Polar Rim to find some amazing animals in this fantastic zoo. You can also take a safari tour and have an adventure in a Nairobi village, a gorilla forest, and the Asian savanna!

Smithsonian National Museum of Natural History, Washington, D.C.
www.mnh.si.edu
Visit this outstanding museum to explore the world's largest collection of natural history. The museum includes some amazing items, from dinosaur bones and giant squids to whale skulls and Moon rocks!

Websites

www.kidsknowit.com
This fun website contains an animal database where you can find pictures and facts about all kinds of animals.

http://kids.nationalgeographic.com/kids/animals
This website is packed full of fascinating facts, fun games, and incredible animal photographs.

http://siwild.si.edu
The "Smithsonian Wild" exhibit highlights the diversity of wildlife that exists in different habitats around the world. View some fantastic images and movies in their online exhibit.

www.unitedstatesfauna.com
Find out everything you need to know about animals that live in the United States. You can investigate some of the most dangerous animals that live here and discover some amazing animal facts.

Index

Animal homes quiz answers

1) B
2) B
3) C
4) C
5) B
6) C
7) B
8) A
9) C
10) B
11) C
12) B